A Rock Can Be...

by Laura Purdie Salas

illustrations by Violeta Dabija

MILLBROOK PRESS • MINNEAPOLIS

To my sister, Patty McKenna, who is
beautiful, steadfast, and strong—
just like a rock! —L.P.S.

To my mother. I love you, and I will
always miss you. —V.D.

Text copyright © 2015 by Laura Purdie Salas
Illustrations copyright © 2015 by Violeta Dabija

Millbrook Press
A division of Lerner Publishing Group, Inc.
241 First Avenue North
Minneapolis, MN 55401 USA

For reading levels and more information, look up this title at www.lernerbooks.com.

Main body text set in GFY Brutus 28/42.
Typeface provided by The Chank Company.

Library of Congress Cataloging-in-Publication Data

Salas, Laura Purdie, author.
    A rock can be . . . / by Laura Purdie Salas ; illustrated by Violeta Dabija.
        pages   cm
    ISBN 978-1-4677-2110-3 (lib. bdg. : alk. paper)
    ISBN 978-1-4677-6297-7 (eBook)
    1. Rocks—Juvenile literature. I. Dabija, Violeta, illustrator. II. Title.
QE432.2.S33 2015
552—dc23   2014009377

Manufactured in the United States of America
1 – DP – 12/31/14

A rock is a rock.

It's sand, pebble, stone.

Each rock tells a story,

a tale all its own.

A rock can be a...

Tall mountain

Park fountain

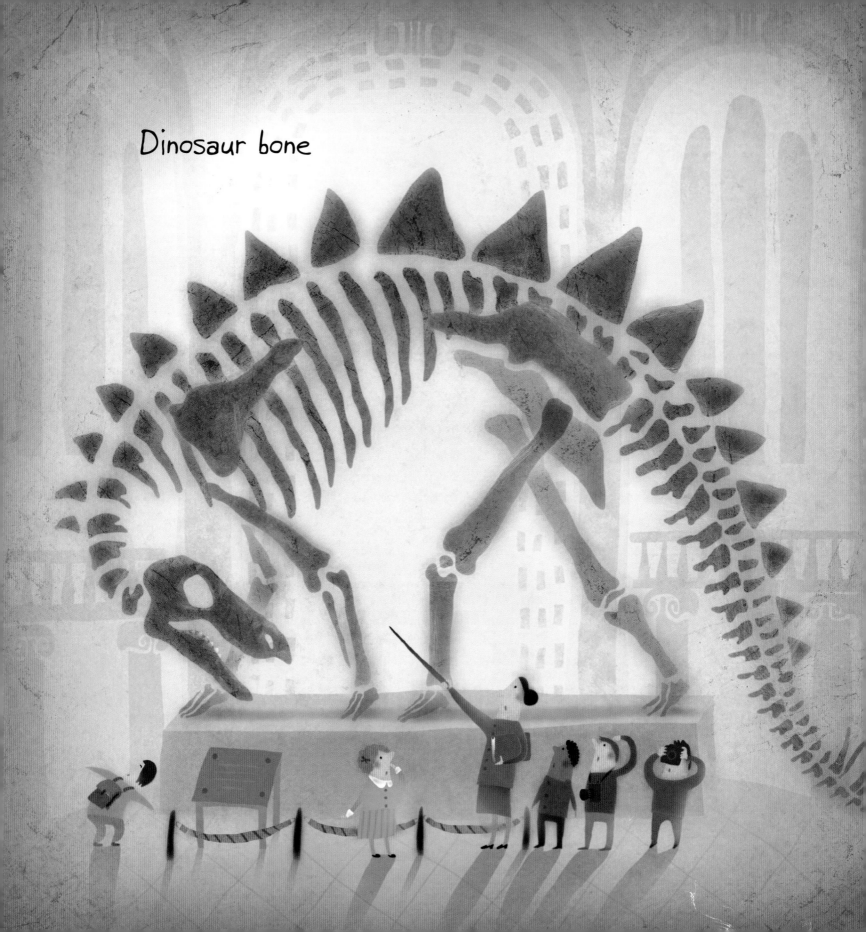

Dinosaur bone

Stepping-stone

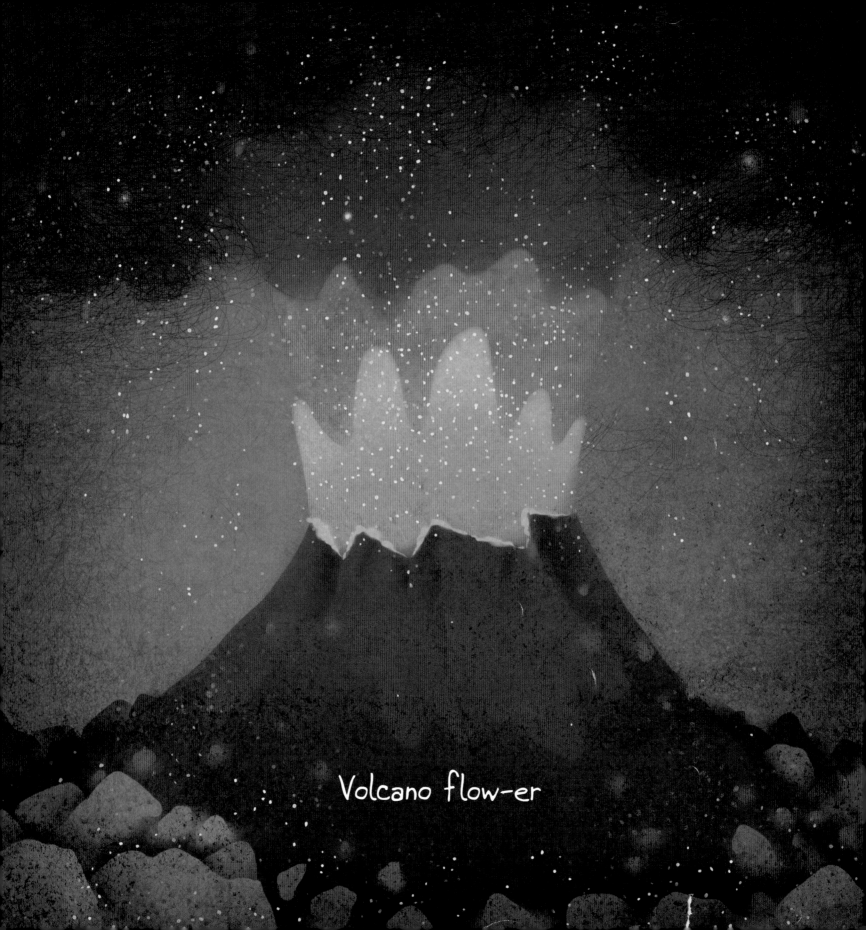

Volcano flow-er

Night glow-er

Lake skimmer

Building trimmer

Hopscotch marker

Fire sparker

A rock is a rock,
our Earth in your hand.
Our world's full of rocks,
some simple, some grand.

A rock can be a...

Seaside home

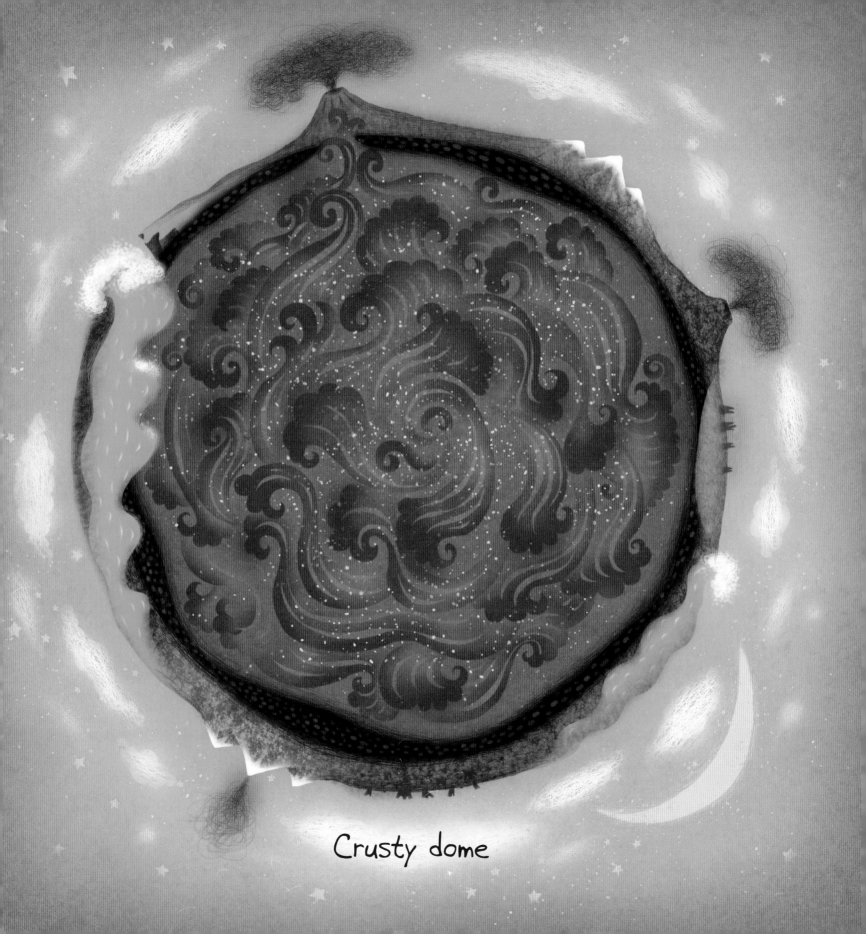

Crusty dome

Desert dune

Harvest moon

Food grinder

Path winder

Harbor protector

Land connector

Sparkling ring

Eagle wing

Book propper

Sheep stopper

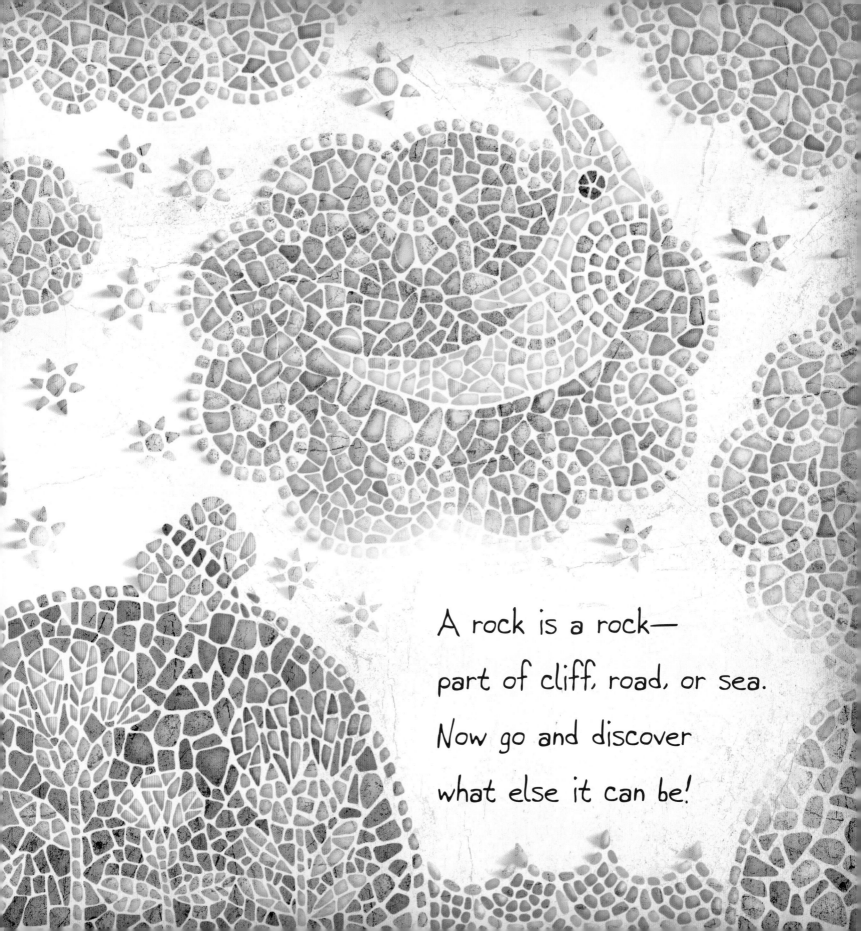

A rock is a rock—
part of cliff, road, or sea.
Now go and discover
what else it can be!

More about Rocks

Rocks are all around us! You probably see rocks lying on the ground every single day. But they don't just lie around. Rocks have lots of important jobs to do. We use rocks for their beauty and their hardness. And sometimes we just like to have fun with them. How do you use rocks?

Tall mountain: Earth's outer layer, or crust, is made of about twelve massive plates of rock. These plates move around very slowly and sometimes bump into one another. When this happens, the rock may gradually crumple up and build toward the sky. That makes a mountain.

Park fountain: Some parks have fancy stone fountains with water flowing, dancing, or bubbling. People often throw pennies into fountains and make a wish.

Dinosaur bone: When an animal dies, if conditions are exactly right, it might become a fossil. If that happens, the animal's bones and teeth very slowly turn into stone. Dinosaurs left behind many bones that became fossils. Copies of these fossils are used to make the dinosaur skeletons in museums.

Stepping-stone: Hard, flat rocks like slate and flagstone make great paths to follow.

Volcano flow-er: Deep inside Earth, it's very hot—hot enough to melt rock! Sometimes, molten rock flows up inside a volcano. Then it erupts as a glowing, burning-hot mixture called lava. When the lava cools off, it hardens into rock.

Night glow-er: Some rocks are phosphorescent. That means they glow in the dark. These rocks and minerals absorb energy from light quickly. Then they release it very slowly. After sundown, you can see them shimmer in the dark.

Lake skimmer: Have you ever skipped a stone across a lake? A flat, round stone works best. If you fling it at just the right angle, it might bounce over the surface of the water. The world record is more than fifty skips.

Building trimmer: Lots of buildings have special details made from carved stone. It might be fancy trim around doors or windows, or it might even be gargoyles guarding the roof.

Hopscotch marker: Hopscotch is a game that really rocks! You use chalk (which is a soft kind of rock) to draw a hopscotch "board" onto pavement. On each turn, you toss a pebble into one of the sections of your board and hop through the other sections without landing on any of the dividing lines.

Fire sparker: Flint is a glassy kind of rock. When flint strikes certain metals, sparks sometimes fly. Long before matches were invented, people scraped flint against steel or iron to start fires.

Seaside home: Not all birds build nests with twigs and grass. Burrowing parrots tunnel out nests in cliffs by the ocean. One colony of more than thirty-five thousand pairs of parrots stretches over 5 miles (8 kilometers) of cliffs in Argentina, a country in South America.

Crusty dome: The rocky plates that make up Earth's crust float on top of the molten, or melted, rock below. When they bump into or slide underneath one another, they can create volcanoes or mountains—and even cause earthquakes.

Desert dune: Some deserts have sand dunes. Those tiny grains of sand started out as larger pieces of rock that broke down over time. Sometimes, wind blows sand into large hills, called dunes.

Harvest moon: The moon's crust is rock, just like Earth's. Each year, the full moon that appears around September 22 is called a harvest moon. Before electricity, farmers sometimes used moonlight to see while they harvested their crops.

Food grinder: Many birds, including chickens, swallow pebbles to help digest their food. The pebbles stay in a special part of the chicken's stomach. When the chicken eats, the rocks jiggle around and help grind up the swallowed food.

Path winder: Have you ever walked on a bumpy gravel road? Gravel is made from rocks broken into small pieces. Sometimes wind and water break bigger rocks into smaller ones. But other times, we use machines to crush rock into gravel.

Harbor protector: A harbor is a pocket of calm water along the coast. A harbor can be formed by a long pile of rocks stretching into the sea, called a breakwater. A breakwater keeps rough waves from coming close to shore and lets boats anchor safely.

Land connector: Stone bridges can help us get from one side of a river to the other. Have you ever crossed a stone bridge?

Sparkling ring: Diamonds form about 100 miles (160 km) underground. Each diamond starts with a chunk of black carbon. Fiery heat and the weight of all the rock above the carbon change it into a diamond over millions of years.

Eagle wing: Sculptors can create anything from rock. They start with a big piece of rock and break away pieces of it using hammers and chisels. Then they use files and smaller tools to shape a statue's details.

Book propper: Because most rocks are heavy, they make great bookends. Marble bookends keep books standing up straight in a row.

Sheep stopper: Walls made out of stone can keep things out or keep things in. The walls of a fort keep attackers out. A stone wall on an old farm keeps sheep in.

Glossary

carbon: a material found in nature. Diamonds are made of carbon.

chisel: a metal tool with a flat, sharp edge used to cut and carve

coast: land near the sea or ocean

colony: a group of animals living together in an area

crust: Earth's rocky outer layer

dinosaur: a type of reptile that lived long ago

earthquake: a movement of parts of Earth's crust that makes the ground shake

fossil: the remains of an animal or a plant from long ago, preserved as rock

harbor: calm, deep water near a coast, where it is safe for ships to dock

gargoyle: a statue of a scary-looking person or animal, usually found on the roof of a building

lava: melted rock that erupts from deep inside Earth and pours out of a volcano

mineral: a material formed by processes in nature and found in the ground

molten: melted by heat

phosphorescent: giving off light without any heat

volcano: a hill or mountain that contains a hole in Earth's crust. When a volcano erupts, rocks and lava pour out of this hole.

Further Reading

Aston, Dianna Hutts. *A Rock Is Lively.* San Francisco: Chronicle Books, 2012.

Christian, Peggy. *If You Find a Rock.* Orlando, FL: Harcourt, 2008.

Rocks and Minerals. Eye Wonder series. London: DK Publishing, 2014.

Tomecek, Steve. *Jump into Science: Rocks and Minerals.* Washington, DC: National Geographic Children's Books, 2010.

Walker, Sally M. *Researching Rocks.* Minneapolis: Lerner Publications, 2013.